Judah

From a sinful man to t

h

People IN THE BIBLE

Paul E. Brown

DayOne

© Day One Publications 2017

ISBN 978-1-84625-575-5

All Scripture quotations, unless stated otherwise, are from the anglicized edition of
the ESV Bible copyright © 2002 Collins, part of HarperCollins Publishers.

British Library Cataloguing in Publication Data available

Published by Day One Publications
Ryelands Road, Leominster, HR6 8NZ
Telephone 01568 613 740 FAX 01568 611 473
email—sales@dayone.co.uk
web site—www.dayone.co.uk

Cover design by Rob Jones, Elk Design
Printed by TJ International

This book began as a sermon on Judah himself but developed as I traced the many references to Judah throughout the Bible. I would like to dedicate the book to the churches in the North West of England, where I have been privileged to preach God's Word.
I am grateful to God for the love and support of my wife, Mary, and would also like to acknowledge the editorial help of Suzanne Mitchell.

Contents

'A book about Judah?' you may be wondering. 'Why Judah, of all people?' It is true that we do not know a great deal about him. He was one of the sons of Jacob, of course, but at first sight he seems to have been someone of very dubious character. His story, such as it is, tends to be overlooked, and he certainly appears to have been overshadowed by his half-brother Joseph. You may be feeling that there cannot be much spiritual benefit in reading about Judah. Yet he experienced a remarkable change of life and character, and left an extraordinary legacy.

Consider these facts. Judah the man is mentioned forty-four times in the Bible. As with the other sons of Jacob—or Israel, as God called him (Gen. 35:10)—a tribe was descended from him. That tribe is mentioned over 170 times. When the nation of Israel was divided, the southern kingdom was called Judah, because that was the dominant tribe in that region. There are nearly 600 references to the kingdom of Judah.

By New Testament times the southern portion of the land was known as Judea, a name which is found nearly fifty times. Even before the time of Christ, the people of this region came to be called Jews after the area to which they belonged. Combining Old Testament and New Testament references and adding words like Jewess and Jewish, these words are found nearly 300 times. There were also other people with the name Judah, probably given it after their ancestor—but we can leave them to one side.

So Judah was the source of close on 1,150 references in the Bible—an astonishing total. He also gave his name to one of the ancient religions of the world—Judaism. More important than any of these things, however, is the fact that it was from the line of Judah that Jesus Christ was born. Yet the man himself has been almost totally ignored. It is time to consider his story.

A troubled family (Gen. 29–37)

It should never have happened, but it did. Jacob loved a woman called Rachel—his cousin, the daughter of his mother's brother (see Gen. 29). He worked for seven years for Uncle Laban in order to marry Rachel, in lieu of a dowry. 'And they seemed to him but a few days because of the love he had for her' (v. 20). At last the wedding day arrived. There was a great feast and much merriment, and in the evening the bride was brought, veiled, to Jacob. In the darkness of the night he took her into his room (or tent). In the morning, when he awoke, he discovered that she was not Rachel, but her older sister Leah!

Not surprisingly, Jacob remonstrated with Laban, 'Why … have you deceived me?' (v. 25). Laban came up with an excuse: 'It is not so done in our country, to give the younger before the firstborn' (v. 26). If this was indeed the case, why had Laban not said so seven years earlier? Genesis 29 tells us that 'Leah's eyes were weak, but Rachel was beautiful in form and appearance' (v. 17). The likelihood is that Laban was fearful that Leah would never get a husband. Moreover, by acting as he did, he gained an extra seven years' labour from his nephew, for after seven days Rachel was also given to Jacob as a wife, with those additional years as a stipulation. In addition, Laban gave each of his daughters a female servant. The fact was that Jacob, a deceiver himself, was getting his comeuppance, but it was to mean a very unhappy home life for the whole family.

Jacob had deceived his own father, Isaac, and had stolen his father's blessing from his older brother, Esau. He had, in part at least, been sent to Laban to get him away from the fury of Esau, who had vowed to kill

Jacob as soon as Isaac died. It is a very sorry story, but God had much to teach Jacob through all that happened to him and his family. Later, Moses was to warn the people of Israel, 'Be sure your sin will find you out' (Num. 32:23). Jacob was proving the reality of this warning. He would find out that his sin would bring disharmony and unhappiness to all the members of his family. All too often, children suffer as a result of the sins and foolishness of their parents.

Almost inevitably we are told that Jacob 'loved Rachel more than Leah' (29:30). It could hardly have been otherwise, for he had not loved Leah at all. The fact that she was surreptitiously given to him as his wife was not likely to engender love for her. In the course of time, Leah began to bear children. The first was Reuben; then, after Simeon and Levi, came the fourth son. She called him Judah, which means 'Praise', for she said, 'This time I will praise the LORD.' These words remind us that these were people who professed faith in God. They were all relatives or descendants of Abraham, and they clearly acknowledged the LORD, the God of Abraham, as their God. We cannot directly compare them to Christian people today, but if we do not learn from them and their faults, we are very foolish. Not every 'Christian' family is the loving, caring family that we expect such families to be.

Rachel became more and more envious of her sister as the years went by and no child was born to her. She cried out petulantly to her husband, 'Give me children, or I shall die!' (30:1). In her extreme desire to have a child, she gave Jacob her servant girl Bilhah to act as a sort of surrogate. Bilhah bore two sons to Jacob, Dan and Naphtali, whom Rachel looked upon as her own. By this time, Leah had ceased bearing children, so she copied Rachel, and two sons, Gad and Asher, were born to her maid Zilpah. Then Leah conceived again and two further sons were born to her, Issachar and Zebulun. Jacob now had a family of ten sons, but with three different mothers. At last, Rachel became pregnant and a son was born, Joseph, to be followed some time later by Benjamin. Twelve sons, four mothers, one father, all living together—a sure-fire recipe for trouble!

The four sons of the servant girls must surely have felt at a disadvantage and it is likely that the other brothers looked down on them. We ought to note that it was of these four that Joseph was later to bring a bad report to his father (Gen. 37:2). It is easy to imagine that they had a 'chip on their shoulders' and as a result were rather careless of their father's flocks. Bilhah and Zilpah, the servant girls, may have felt that their sons were not treated as equals. They themselves were surely very conscious of their position and might have felt that they had been used in the tension between Rachel and Leah.

We are told that Jacob loved Joseph 'more than any other of his sons, because he was the son of his old age' (37:3)—though, of course, that was even more true of Benjamin. It is often said that Jacob showed favouritism to Joseph. This is true, but it is a rather Western and perhaps modern way of expressing it. Not only was Joseph the son of his beloved wife Rachel, but when at last he was born, Jacob must have looked upon him almost as his heir. After all, but for the deceit of Laban, Jacob would simply have married Rachel, and Joseph would truly have had the status of firstborn. When Joseph had his first dream (37:5–8), it must have seemed to the brothers that this was simply confirming what Jacob's attitude and actions had appeared to suggest. The second dream went even further, with Jacob himself bowing down to Joseph. Jacob obviously thought that there was more to the dreams than appeared on the surface, as he 'kept the saying in mind' (37:11).

It was in this troubled family, with its many tensions and cross-currents of emotion, that Judah was brought up. He was surely a rather mixed-up kid himself and doubtless shared his brothers' hatred of Joseph. Though not born from one of the servant girls, he had no particular status as the fourth son of Leah. His unimportance is emphasized by the fact that he is not mentioned by name until he suggested that Joseph could be sold to the Ishmaelites. It appears that originally he was quite content with the scheme to murder Joseph (37:18). There is a certain ambiguity about his words in verses 26–27: 'What profit is it if we kill our brother and conceal his blood? Come, let us sell him to the Ishmaelites, and let not our hand be upon him, for he is our brother, our own flesh.' A lot depends on whether we emphasize the word 'profit'. Was he simply thinking that, by selling Joseph, they would get money, which otherwise they would not; or do his words 'and let not our hand be upon him, for he is our brother, our own flesh' indicate some sense of family feeling? It is difficult to believe that these words do not show some sense of kinship and responsibility. To kill your 'own flesh' is an aggravation of murder. Better to get the money and not have the guilt of fratricide on their consciences.

Jacob was the grandson of Abraham, the man of faith. More importantly, Abraham had been called by God and told that his descendants would be as numerous as the stars in the sky and the sand on the seashore. He was the man through whom the nations of the world would be blessed. Abraham was called the 'friend of God' (James 2:23) and became known as the father of the nation of Israel. He was not perfect, of course, but his faith and trust in God were outstanding. Isaac, his son, was a man of God too. God revealed himself to him and gave him promises (Gen. 26:24–25). However, he and his wife Rebekah each had their favourite son. Isaac's favourite was Esau, while Rebekah's was Jacob. It led to an unhappy family life and had serious consequences. Seeds were sown by them that would lead to bitter fruit in the next generation.

It is sadly not unusual for spirituality and godliness to diminish as children grow up and succeed their parents. It is easy for children brought up in Christian homes to take their faith for granted and to forget that each generation has to trust God and follow his Word carefully. As a result, they all too easily slip away gradually from their initial profession. The faults and failings of parents come to be imitated in the next generation and are often used as an excuse for the further declension of their children.

The remarkable fact, however, is that God still had his covenant purposes which would be fulfilled through Abraham's children. The way Jacob was treated by Laban was used by God to humble Jacob and to teach him vividly that, although he could deceive, others could do so better than he could, and with even more unhappy consequences. Eventually, through much fear and distress, he was brought to Bethel, where God appeared to him, blessed him and changed his name to Israel (35:9–15). Through heartache and sorrow he came to the place where he would confess 'The God before whom my fathers Abraham and Isaac walked, the God who has been my shepherd all my life long to this day' (48:15).

Two truths must be held in tension. On the one hand, those who are in covenant with God are under obligation to walk humbly before him and follow after holiness of life. On the other hand, their obedience is not necessarily essential to God bringing his purposes to pass. The wonderful thing is that God is able to work out his plans of grace through people who are far from perfect. Indeed, if he were to wait until we were all that we ought to be, his purposes would come to a halt. We must emphasize the first truth: we dare not complacently say that God will work out his will anyway. On the other hand, we should be truly thankful that he does use people who are very far from being suitable and adequate—the Jacobs and Judahs of this world.

The turning point (Gen. 38)

Genesis 38 switches the spotlight on to Judah and reveals first of all a man who was not concerned about belonging to a godly line. He went away and left his brothers. We are not told why he did so, other than that he had become friendly with a man called Hirah and it seems he went to stay with him. This man is described as an Adullamite, though whether he was living in Adullam or not is not explicitly mentioned. At any rate, Judah was away from the rest of his family. The nationality of Hirah is not given, but the passage seems to mark him off from the Canaanites. Whether he was a suitable friend for Judah becomes rather doubtful as we read through this chapter. Friends can be a great help and blessing, but they can sometimes be a means of leading people away from God and the paths of righteousness.

It was while he was with Hirah, away from his father and family, that 'Judah saw the daughter of a certain Canaanite whose name was Shua' (38:2). 'Shua' was the name of the 'certain Canaanite' (cf. 1 Chr. 2:3: 'Bath-shua' simply means 'daughter of Shua'); the name of the lady is not even given. The emphasis of these early verses is solely on the fact that Judah married the daughter of a Canaanite. His great-grandfather, Abraham, had been very concerned that his God-given and God-preserved son Isaac should not marry a wife 'from the daughters of the Canaanites' (24:3). The Canaanites were a particularly evil and idolatrous people, though the Lord bore with their sins until their iniquity was complete (15:16).

In order to find a suitable wife for his son, Abraham had sent his servant to Nahor in Mesopotamia, where Abraham's relatives were living. In due course Rebekah was brought back and became Isaac's wife. Isaac and Rebekah had twins, Esau and Jacob. When Esau, the firstborn, was forty years old, he took two wives, Judith and Basemath, both of whom were Hittites. The Hittites were a tribe that can be included under the general name of Canaanites. We are told of these two that 'they made life bitter for Isaac and Rebekah' (26:35). The story then became more complicated. For our purposes we can simply note that Rebekah said to Isaac, 'I loathe my life because of the Hittite women. If Jacob marries one of the Hittite women like these, one of the women of the land, what good will my life be to me?' (27:46).

As a result of what his wife said, 'Isaac called Jacob and blessed him and directed him, "You must not take a wife from the Canaanite women"' (28:1). So Jacob was sent to Laban to find a wife from among his relatives, and this led to what we have already seen: he ended up being married to both Leah and Rachel. It is difficult to believe that Judah had no knowledge of the reason why his father had been sent to Laban, nor of the case of his grandfather Isaac. He would also have known about the incident concerning his sister Dinah, which is recounted in chapter 34. In spite of all that had happened in the past, the narrative in chapter 38 simply tells us that Judah 'saw the daughter of a certain Canaanite ... He took her and went in to her, and she conceived and bore a son' (vv. 2–3). The sheer brevity of this seems to underline that he was visually and powerfully attracted to this woman and, without any qualms, simply took her as his wife. Perhaps Judah had left home so that he could choose his own wife, without Jacob having any say in the matter.

Judah's wife bore two more boys and gradually the years went by. In the course of time, Judah took a wife for his eldest son, Er; her name was Tamar. There is no indication of her nationality (though the likelihood is that she too was a Canaanite), but it is interesting that Judah found her for his son. There was no going off as Judah himself had done and marrying without parental consent. Judah's firstborn was 'wicked in the sight of the LORD', following, perhaps, in the footsteps of his father and mother. The LORD terminated his life, but he left no heir.

As the custom was in those days—a custom that would continue later in the nation of Israel—the second son, Onan, was then given to Tamar in marriage to raise up an heir for his brother. Onan, however, knowing that the firstborn would be considered not his but his deceased brother's, took steps to ensure that Tamar would not conceive. But this breach of his responsibility to his brother and Tamar displeased the LORD, and he died also. The end of Genesis 37 highlighted Jacob's deep grief over the loss of Joseph. By contrast, Judah does not appear to have been much moved by the loss of his two sons. His was a harder heart than his father's.

Shelah, Judah's youngest son, was not yet fully adult, so Judah advised Tamar to go home and remain as a widow in her father's house until Shelah had finished growing up. However, the truth was that Judah had no intention of giving his youngest son to Tamar. The Bible says that 'he feared that he would die, like his brothers' (38:11). Whether he thought that the deaths of the first two brothers were in some way Tamar's responsibility or not, he had decided that it was better to be on the safe side and to find a different wife for Shelah. So when Shelah was fully grown there was no move to give him to Tamar, and she realized that he was reneging on his promise.

What took place after this is not pleasant to consider, but it reflects the moral standards of many in those days—and, indeed, the moral standards of many today also. Judah's wife died, and when the days of mourning were over he went with his friend Hirah to the sheep-shearing in a place called Timnah. The fact that his wife had died made him more vulnerable to what happened next. Tamar was told that Judah would be passing by. By this time, she had realized that Shelah was not going to be given to her in marriage. He was now fully grown and there had been no move to bring them together. She was in an unenviable position, dependent on her father, who doubtless did not want to have to look after a widowed daughter.

She knew that she had been wronged by her father-in-law, Judah, and she determined to see if she could have a son and heir by him. So she dressed herself as a cult prostitute, with a veil over her face so that she could not be recognized, and sat by the roadside outside a town that Judah would pass through. The religion of the Canaanites was based on fertility, and cult prostitutes were an integral part of the fertility rites that took place—though this also provided an excuse for immoral behaviour. It may be that sheep-shearing was a time when such rites were involved, for wool was a valuable commodity. It was also a time of rejoicing, and it is likely that there was plenty of alcoholic refreshment available. Matthew Henry has a very up-to-date comment, though the language is old-fashioned: 'Times of jollity oft prove times of temptation, particularly to the sin of uncleanness.'[1]

When Judah saw the disguised Tamar, he turned aside to her and asked to have intercourse with her. She agreed to this, provided that he give her a young goat in payment. As he did not have a goat with him, he gave her his signet ring, cord and staff as a pledge that he would bring the goat later. Once he had gone on his way, she went home and changed back into her widow's clothing. Judah then sent the goat by his friend, Hirah, but of course he was not able to find the prostitute. Nor did anyone know that there had ever been one in that place. Doubtless, Judah soon forgot all about what had happened.

Three months later he was told that his daughter-in-law was pregnant. He was furious and said, 'Bring her out, and let her be burned' (v. 24). This is the more terrible when we remember that there was an unborn, and therefore entirely innocent, baby that would have been killed as well as its mother. This brutal savagery suggests that he had been strongly influenced by Canaanite culture, which was not only immoral but also viciously cruel. When some men from Judah came to bring her out—

presumably to condemn her and put her to death—she sent the signet ring, the cord and staff back to Judah with the message, 'By the man to whom these belong, I am pregnant' (v. 25).

It seems as if, when Judah saw the evidence of his sin and realized what had happened, his world was suddenly turned upside down. 'She is more righteous than I, since I did not give her to my son Shelah,' he said (v. 26). This was the turning point in Judah's life. The words he uttered are astonishing. He recognized his own guilt in his treatment of her. In spite of what she had done in seducing him, he acknowledged that she was more righteous than he had been. At the heart of what he meant must surely be this: he had utterly condemned her for immorality and had been about to have her killed by a most terrible death, yet it was by his own immoral act that she had become pregnant. He saw himself as he had never seen himself before. He had been about to kill someone for an act which he had committed—after all, he could have walked on by when he saw her by the roadside. If she was wrong to put temptation in his way, it had required him to give way to temptation for the actual act of sin to take place.

There was, however, more to it than this. Tamar was part of Judah's family; she had been married to two of his sons. It was she who should have provided an heir to carry on the family line—an heir who would also have provided for her and her husband when they reached old age. Yet Judah had summarily despatched her back to her father and it had become evident that, in spite of what he had said, Judah was not going to give his son Shelah to her in marriage. This would mean that Shelah would be married to someone else who would give birth to the heir. Tamar was simply being written out of the script! Her action, sinful though it was, actually secured an heir for Judah and secured her place in the family. No wonder Judah said, 'She is more righteous than I.' He had been rejecting all responsibility for her, but now she had found a way of regaining the place from which she should never have been expelled. Moreover, she had provided him with an heir as well.

It may seem surprising to us that Judah should have said, 'She is more righteous than I.' Would it not have been more correct to say, 'My guilt is far greater than hers', or 'Her sin is nothing compared to mine'? In what way was it appropriate to speak of her as 'righteous'? The answer seems to lie here: Tamar had been clearly rejected by Judah, but she was his daughter-in-law. By consenting to marry Er she had taken certain obligations upon herself. She had been expected to provide an heir, not just for Er, but also for Judah. She had become a member, and an important member, of the family; in due time she would have been expected to help care for Judah and his wife, if she had lived, in their old age.

Judah might have thrown off his obligations to her, but she had remembered her obligations to him and the family. Back in her father's house she did not seek another husband, which surely must have been at least a possibility. She had no intention of becoming a real cult prostitute, which other women in her position might have considered to be the only way of earning a living. She may have adopted an expedient that was sinful, but her ultimate intentions were righteous, and this was what Judah recognized.

To return to Judah, this event must also have reminded him of the past. He had been complicit in expelling someone else from the family. Perhaps his conscience had somewhat troubled him when it seemed as if his brothers were going to kill Joseph. At any rate, it had been his idea to sell Joseph as a slave. He had been just as concerned to get Joseph out of his life as he was to do the same to Tamar. And he had seen how his father's heart had been broken as his sons had shown him Joseph's robe, torn and spattered with goat's blood (37:29–35). Possibly part of his reason for leaving his brothers and the family home (38:1) had been a troubled conscience from seeing the dreadful sorrow he and his brothers had inflicted on Jacob.

Not only did Judah say that Tamar was more righteous than he, but he also went on to acknowledge explicitly his own fault: 'since I did not give her to my son Shelah'. Here he was owning up to his fault to those who came bringing the evidence that showed he was responsible for Tamar's pregnancy. He had gone back to the beginning, to the cause which brought about Tamar's action. What she had done was wrong, but it was he who had put her in the position that led her to act as she did. He did not try to excuse himself. He did not blame her for putting temptation in his way. He frankly confessed before others that he had been in the wrong. We might have thought that Judah was too hardened a man to do this, but we can thank God that this was not so.

Judah's confession was made in the presence not only of the men he had sent: God is the great observer of all that goes on in this world. He sees and hears everything. This open confession of guilt was therefore in his ears and before his eyes. It quite clearly came straight from Judah's heart. Whether, at some time after this, there was explicit confession before God or the offering of sacrifice to him, we do not know, but this honest admission of his responsibility and failure was surely accepted by God. We all fall into sin, but we often do not find it so easy to make a full and frank confession, either to those we have offended or to the Lord himself. We try to make excuses and, if possible, shuffle off some of the responsibility. Judah could have done the latter, but it is to his credit that he did not.

We all too easily do what Judah did not do. We try to hide behind the other person's fault. It is true that Tamar had sinned, but Judah acknowledged that it was his prior sin that had brought that about. He had been responsible for putting her into the position that had led to her adopting the extreme measure that she took. In a heated argument, two people are very often both at fault in what they say, but usually it is one of them who has started the argument or is the cause of the argument. We must learn to face up to ourselves; to go to the beginning and confess if the original fault is ours.

The narrative goes on to include this sentence: 'And he did not know her again' (v. 26). The likelihood is that after this, Judah took Tamar back into his own home and became responsible for her welfare. After all, the twins that were born were his sons. Moreover, this sentence would scarcely have been necessary if she had returned to her own father. In any case, her father would not have wanted to have responsibility for her two children. So we can be fairly sure that Judah lived up to his responsibilities. It was not enough simply to confess his sin: his sin had brought certain obligations upon himself—as sin can often do—and he fulfilled them. Throughout history, it became known that Perez was his son and his heir. We might also note that his action had the effect of sidelining Shelah. By trying to keep him from Tamar, he ended up cutting him out as his own heir, and we simply do not know what happened to him. Sin so often has unintended consequences, and many in this world suffer from this form of collateral damage.

From this time on Judah became a different person—although we are not actually told that. We do not find Judah making any promise to act differently in the future, nor any comment about a great change of heart and behaviour. However, we learn that he became different simply by looking at what happened later on. This is always the best form of evidence. People sometimes make great promises about being different in the future and give passionate testimony to a change in their lives, but it is the reality that proves whether or not this is so. Words have their place, but they can prove to be empty. It is new attitudes and a new life that constitute the evidence that counts.

This is a difficult passage to meditate on because an act of sin lies at its heart. Yet we have to recognize that we live in a sinful world. As we have seen already, God may bring his purposes to pass in spite of—indeed, sometimes through—the evil desires and deeds of men and women. This does not justify sin: it magnifies the grace of God! We cannot justify what Tamar did, even if we can sympathize with her predicament and understand why she acted as she did. Nor can we excuse Judah, but we can learn some useful lessons from him.

As is too often the case, Judah had gone from bad to worse. The seeds of all sins are in human hearts, and when sin is not restrained deterioration goes on apace, as it did with Judah. Sometimes God allows people to go far into sin as a means to stop them short when they realize just what they have done and how lost they are. Judah had to face himself, his fury and cruelty, his careless attitude to the welfare and feelings of other people, and the influence upon him of Canaanite ways and morals. By the grace of God he confessed that he was a sinner—a woman who had prostituted herself was more righteous than he!

Judah came to see himself as he really was while he was still in this life and with time before him to live in a very different way. It is a great mercy—even if it comes as it did for Judah—to come face to face with ourselves while we are still alive and there is opportunity to repent and seek grace from God to change and live differently in the future. Paul, in Romans 3:19, speaks of 'every mouth' being 'stopped' when the whole world is held accountable to God. On the day of judgement no one will have any excuse; all who are condemned will know that their judgement is just and right; they will see themselves as they never really saw themselves while in this world. To have that conviction brought home in the present is never a pleasant experience, but it causes us to exclaim, 'What must I do to be saved?' This then becomes the most urgent problem in the world, for which the Bible provides the answer: 'Believe in the Lord Jesus, and you will be saved' (Acts 16:30–31).

We must also briefly consider the bigger picture at this point. Tamar bore twins. The first to be born was Perez, who became Judah's heir. His name occurs a few times in the Old Testament in genealogies, but we can easily miss his significance until we find his name occurring in Matthew 1. There we read this:

The book of the genealogy of Jesus Christ, the son of David, the son of Abraham. Abraham was the father of Isaac, and Isaac the father of Jacob, and Jacob the father of Judah and his brothers, and Judah the father of Perez and Zerah by Tamar, and Perez the father of Hezron ... (vv. 1–3)

How astonishing: the direct line from Abraham to Jesus Christ ran through Judah and Tamar and Perez, and Tamar is actually mentioned by name, thus drawing attention to her! This is the amazing grace of God, who brings good out of evil and carries out his gracious purposes in a sinful world through flawed and guilty sinners!

NOTE

1 Matthew Henry, *An Exposition of the Old and New Testaments* (3 vols, 19th cent.). Note on Genesis 38:12–22.

Judah and Jacob
(Gen. 43:1–44:14)

During the years that saw Judah get married and the events that we have just considered, Joseph was in Egypt. He had passed through many difficulties before being raised up as the second in the kingdom after Pharaoh himself (41:37–45). By this time he was thirty years of age (41:46). He owed his position to the fact that he had been able, with God's help, to interpret the dreams of Pharaoh. These had indicated that there were going to be seven years of plentiful harvests followed by seven years of famine. Pharaoh saw that the Spirit of God was in Joseph and appointed him to prepare for the years of famine. During the seven years when there was plenty of food available, Joseph gathered great stores in readiness for what was to come (41:47–49).

When these famine years arrived they affected the land of Canaan as well as Egypt, thus including Jacob and his growing family—or small clan, as it was by this time. Ten brothers were sent to Egypt to buy grain, but Jacob would not send Benjamin, his other son by Rachel, with them. When the brothers arrived Joseph recognized them, but they had no idea that he was their brother whom they had sold into slavery. Genesis 42 tells what happened. Joseph accused his brothers of being spies who were taking advantage of the famine to search out the state of the land. This led them to explain that they were all brothers, mentioning that one was lost and the youngest was still at home. The upshot was that the brothers were given grain and sent home, but Simeon was kept as a hostage. When they needed to return for more supplies, they were to bring Benjamin with them to prove the truth of what they had told Joseph. Only then would Simeon be released.

The brothers returned home to Jacob, who was horrified at the turn of events and vowed that Benjamin would never be given into their hands to take to Egypt. But the time came when they had eaten up all the grain they had brought from Egypt. Jacob said to his sons, 'Go again, buy us a little food' (43:2), and at this point it is Judah who steps into the picture (v. 3). It is intriguing that it is Judah who speaks to his father, not Reuben. When the brothers first returned home and told Jacob that 'the man' had said that Benjamin must go with them on any future visit, it was Reuben who spoke up: 'Kill my two sons if I do not bring him back to you. Put him in my hands, and I will bring him back to you' (42:37). But Reuben appeared to be silent now that the time to go had actually come. Or it may simply be that Judah got in first. At any rate, Judah took the initiative at this point.

Judah's insistence that Benjamin must go to Egypt with the rest of them or they will not go down themselves anticipates what is shortly to come (43:8–10). His words to his father on this occasion show a very different relationship between father and son from that of the past. Their relationship is clearly closer now, and Jacob listens to Judah. Although Judah has emphasized that Benjamin must go down with them if they are to get food again, there is no repetition of Jacob's words of 42:38: 'My son shall not go down with you.' Rather, Jacob seems to have accepted the inevitability of all ten sons going: 'Why did you treat me so badly as to tell the man that you had another brother?' (43:6).

Judah has not finished, however. 'And Judah said to Israel his father, "Send the boy with me, and we will arise and go ... I will be a pledge of his safety. From my hand you shall require him. If I do not bring him back to you and set him before you, then let me bear the blame for ever."' Here is a man who does not simply have a better relationship with his father, but who has undergone a profound change of heart. The one who callously suggested selling his brother into slavery and joined in a deception that led his father to believe his son was dead and plunged him into grief, is now pledging his own life on the safe return of the second son of Rachel. His words here show us just what a change took place in him as a result of Tamar's action and the way this forced him to face himself: 'She is more righteous than I.' Implicit in the narrative is the wonderful grace of God that, in a sinful world, and through human sin, can nevertheless effect such a complete turnaround. God has taken away a heart of stone and replaced it with a heart of flesh: a heart that is sensitive, feeling, loving and self-sacrificing (Ezek. 36:26).

We must remember that all this time (probably about a year; see 45:11) Simeon had been in prison in Egypt. Judah could not know in what conditions Simeon was being kept, nor how he was faring—or whether in fact he was still alive. After all, how well would prisoners have been looked after in a time of general famine? None of the brothers could be quite sure why the man who they did not know was Joseph was so emphatic that their brother must be brought down. He was obviously very suspicious of them; would those suspicions be put to rest when another brother came with them? How would the man know for sure that it was their brother? Judah did not know the future—indeed, could not know it; but he was willing to put his life on the line in order to provide the food they all needed to stay alive. If Joseph, by God's grace, kept many people alive (50:20), Judah, too, played his part in saving a family of more than sixty-six persons from starvation (46:26).

Jacob bowed his head to accept the inevitable: 'If it must be so, then do this … Take also your brother, and arise, go again to the man' (43:11, 13). Jacob was also a man who had learnt much about himself and his God through hard experience. If the experience of Joseph's disappearance and, as he understood it, his death, plus the loss of Simeon in prison and the proposal that Benjamin must be part of a second visit to Egypt, had caused him great distress of mind, he was still at heart a man of faith in the God of his fathers. So although he took steps to appease 'the man', his final words to his sons were these: 'May God Almighty grant you mercy before the man, and may he send back your other brother and Benjamin. And as for me, if I am bereaved of my children, I am bereaved.' Those last words seem despondent, but they also indicate a submission to the will of God Almighty. Jacob did not know what the outcome was going to be. He prayed to the God he knew, who had helped him and blessed him in the past (35:9–15). All things were in God's hands. Jacob had already learned that God's ways can be strange and disconcerting for those who trust him. He did not understand the present situation, but he knew what to pray for and he left the rest in God's hands. Few of us have passed through such deep waters as he did. Few of us trust God and rest in his will as we should.

The next phase in the story is well known (43:19–44:13). The ten brothers went down to Egypt. Joseph made a feast for them and brought Simeon out of prison to join them. Their sacks were filled with food and their money was returned to them, but Joseph's steward was instructed to put Joseph's silver cup in the top of Benjamin's sack. After they had departed and gone a short way, the steward was sent after them to see if one of them had stolen the cup. It was discovered in Benjamin's sack; so they all returned in great distress and 'Judah and his brothers came to Joseph's house' (44:14). It was time for Judah to live up to his promise to his father.

Judah and Joseph (44:14–45:28)

O n their first visit to Egypt for food, Joseph had accused the brothers of being spies. They were to bring Benjamin with them the next time they came to Egypt in order to demonstrate the truthfulness of their story. Then he would release Simeon to them (42:6–20). This turn of events led the brothers to recognize the hand of God behind the way things were going. Genesis 42:21 tells us that they said to each other, 'In truth we are guilty concerning our brother, in that we saw the distress of his soul, when he begged us and we did not listen. That is why this distress has come upon us.' Later, when they found their money replaced in their sacks, they said, 'What is this that God has done to us?' (42:28). The guilt they felt over the way they had treated Joseph all those years earlier had come to the surface. They could see that God was doing something strange with them, though they did not understand what it was.

We have to keep that in mind as we consider the second visit: the doleful return of the brothers to Joseph's house. Judah now becomes the spokesman for the rest: 'What shall we say to my lord? What shall we speak? Or how can we clear ourselves? God has found out the guilt of your servants; behold, we are my lord's servants, both we and he also in whose hand the cup has been found' (44:16). On the surface, this is Judah speaking on behalf of them all and accepting blame for what it appears Benjamin has done. It looks as if he is saying that they all knew what had been done and are therefore all guilty and will all have to accept servitude to Joseph.

Joseph, of course, knows better, and so he replies, 'Far be it from me that I should do so! Only the man in whose hand the cup was found shall be my servant. But as for you, go up in peace to your father' (v. 17).

There is a terrible irony in those last words. How could they go in peace to their father if Benjamin was not with them? They had faced their father once and lied to him about the disappearance of Joseph. They had seen his terrible distress; they knew only too well what it would mean if they turned up again without the second of Rachel's sons. It was something that could not be contemplated. However, before we go on to consider what Judah said next, we must go back and reconsider the words we have already seen: 'God has found out the guilt of your servants.' Judah knew—they all knew—that the chickens were coming home to roost. They had sold one son of Rachel into slavery and made up a story and evidence to suggest that the boy must be dead. Now God had put them into the position where it looked as if they would have to return to Jacob and tell him the second son was lost to him as well. Their sin had found them out; their guilt was heavy in their hearts; whatever could they do? What could Judah possibly say that would save the day?

What comes next is the longest speech that is recorded in the book of Genesis apart from Jacob's prophecy in chapter 49, and that, of course, looks at each of his sons in turn. Judah's words are actually some of the most important in the whole Bible. They reveal the heart of a man in a way that few other passages do. They show so clearly the amazing change that had come over the Judah whose character appeared earlier in the narrative. It is difficult to read his words with sensitivity and empathy and not to feel tears coming into one's eyes. Here are words that flow from a humble and contrite heart.

First of all, we notice the respectful way that Judah spoke to Joseph: 'Oh, my lord, please let your servant speak a word in my lord's ears, and let not your anger burn against your servant, for you are like Pharaoh himself' (44:18). We would expect this, of course; it would be foolish to be disrespectful to a man in such a position. And yet it is quite clear that these are not simply the right words with a right attitude put on for the occasion. There is a ring of sincerity all through Judah's plea to Joseph. He is very clear in explaining the exact position that he and his brothers are in, and, in particular, he speaks of Jacob in a moving and affecting manner: 'We have a father, an old man, and a young brother, the child of his old age. His brother is dead, and he alone is left of his mother's children, and his father loves him.' This is an astonishing statement; wasn't it because Jacob had loved Joseph that his brothers had hated him? Now Judah speaks with perfect understanding of his father and the inevitable love he felt for Benjamin. What more natural than for Jacob to love his youngest son, the son of his beloved Rachel?

And so Judah continues: 'Then you said to your servants, "Bring him down to me, that I may set my eyes on him." We said to my lord, "The boy cannot leave his father, for if he should leave his father, his father would die"' (vv. 21–22). To travel to Egypt was, in itself, at least potentially dangerous. Judah knew with what pain and anxiety Jacob must have said 'Goodbye' to Benjamin. He knew what Jacob must have been thinking: 'I once sent my older son, Joseph, to his brothers, and he never came back. I dare not risk the life of Benjamin.' And yet he had no choice; without adequate food they would all die. Judah may also have felt that Jacob was suspicious of his other sons. Had they been involved in the disappearance of Joseph? Their bitter hostility towards him could not have been hidden. Perhaps during all the years since Joseph's disappearance Jacob had harboured a thought he dared not express and even tried to suppress: his own sons had done away with Joseph.

Judah understood it all, and his words imply his feeling for his father. What he did not know was that it was Joseph himself who was there listening to him, understanding the situation in exactly the same way.

Judah is telling the story as it was to Joseph in order to try to help 'the man'—as he thought him to be—to understand the situation and be sympathetic to the brothers and especially to their father. And so he goes on to explain how they had persuaded their father to let his youngest son go with them to Egypt, recounting the words that Jacob used: 'Then your servant my father said to us, "You know that my wife bore me two sons. One left me, and I said, Surely he has been torn to pieces, and I have never seen him since. If you take this one also from me, and harm happens to him, you will bring down my grey hairs in evil to Sheol"' (vv. 27–29). Both in verse 24 and in verse 27 Judah says 'my father' rather than use 'our father' as we might expect. That personal pronoun speaks volumes, and he will use it five times more in the next paragraph. There is an unmistakable relationship of sympathy and affection on the part of Judah for his elderly father. How different from the unfeeling man of years before!

All this was merely introductory. Judah continues, 'Now therefore, as soon as I come to your servant my father, and the boy is not with us, then, as his life is bound up in the boy's life, as soon as he sees that the boy is not with us, he will die, and your servants will bring down the grey hairs of your servant our father with sorrow to Sheol' (vv. 30–31). But why does he say, 'as soon as I come', rather than 'as soon as we come'? The answer follows immediately—and here Judah is coming to the heart of what he wants to say and the appeal he will make to Joseph:

For your servant became a pledge of safety for the boy to my father, saying, 'If I do not bring him back to you, then I shall bear the blame before my father all my life.' Now therefore, please let your servant remain instead of the boy as a servant to my lord, and let the boy go back with his brothers. For how can I go back to my father if the boy is not with me? I fear to see the evil that would find my father. (vv. 32–34)

We shall have to delay considering the effect that those words had on Joseph while we look at them more closely. This man speaking is the one who was responsible for Joseph having been sold into slavery. He had no thought for his father then; now, however, his concern for his father is overwhelmingly clear. Now he is willing to become a servant himself, if only 'the man' will accept him instead of his youngest brother. He himself would rather be 'sold' into Egypt than allow this to happen to Benjamin. He has made a solemn pledge to care for this brother and ensure that he returns home, whatever the cost to himself. He will substitute himself in order that his brother may go free. In his own small way he displays the same attitude that the Son of God showed when he came into the world to become a substitute, in order that his brothers and sisters might go free. The same self-sacrificing spirit is found in this Old Testament man: a spirit the very antithesis of that which he had showed earlier in his life. Small wonder that Joseph could not control himself when he heard what Judah had to say (45:1)!

We can see quite clearly from this eloquent appeal that Judah had become the moral leader of his brothers. Reuben had long ago forfeited his position as the eldest son and the one who was fit to represent the family (see 35:22). When it came to convincing Jacob that Benjamin must go with them to Egypt, Judah had been the one who took the lead and persuaded Jacob to let him go. When it came to appealing to Joseph on behalf of Benjamin—and Jacob's well-being too—it was Judah who did the talking. The other brothers were quite content to let him speak; they clearly respected him, his wisdom and his judgement. They were probably very glad that he was willing to take the role that he did. Who would want to be the spokesman in a tricky situation like that?

Proverbs 16:23 says, 'The heart of the wise makes his speech judicious and adds persuasiveness to his lips.' By this standard Judah had learnt wisdom and gained a wise heart. Earlier in the same chapter in Proverbs we read, 'When a man's ways please the LORD, he makes even his enemies to be at peace with him' (v. 7). Judah's ways had changed radically and without doubt were now pleasing to the LORD. In fact, if Judah had not changed and if his brothers had still had the same attitude that they had showed to Joseph years before, Joseph would have seemed a fearsome adversary to them when he made himself known. As it was, Judah's words went straight to Joseph's heart and Joseph was won over by the new attitude they revealed. Proverbs 18:16 says, 'A man's gift makes room for him and brings him before the great.' 'Gift' here probably refers to a bribe, yet the verse is also true in another sense. Those who have gifts of sincerity, wisdom, spiritual grace and humility find that they are enabled to speak for others and make peace in difficult situations. God is glorified by a life that is respected for its transparency and goodness.

Joseph was completely overcome by Judah's words and the attitude that he showed, and he broke down in tears (Gen. 45:1–2). Here was the man who had been responsible for selling him into slavery offering himself as a slave if only Joseph would let Benjamin go free! Joseph sent away all the Egyptians who were with him so that he could reveal to his brothers who he was. Not surprisingly, they were 'dismayed' (v. 3) at this revelation, but he showed quite clearly that he accepted them, telling them that they, Jacob and the whole family must come down into Egypt because there were still five more years of famine to come (v. 11). The brothers took some time to be convinced: not that this was really Joseph, but that he was going to treat them well. Eventually they were able to talk with him (v. 15); their feelings of astonishment and fear had subsided. Joseph, too, put all that had happened over the years into its proper perspective: 'And now do not be distressed or angry with yourselves because you sold me here, for God sent me before you to preserve life' (v. 5). Amazing words—but he evidently recognized that they were truly sorry for what they had done to him. 'And God sent me before you to preserve for you a remnant on earth, and to keep alive for you many survivors. So it was not you who sent me here, but God' (vv. 7–8).

Even without these words we would be able to deduce the truth of what Joseph said here. In spite of the guilt of Judah and his brothers, through the ups and downs of life, God had been at work. It was he who brought Judah face to face with himself and changed him into the man he became. It was God who had been preserving and moulding Joseph through the tumultuous years in Egypt. In fact, the Lord had a long-term strategy which will become plain as we follow the story further.

It is often not easy for us to see the hand of God behind the events of our own lives, yet it is important for us to realize that God is always at work—through individuals, through churches, in spite of the sins and shortcomings of his own people—bringing to pass his own sovereign purposes. However, there are times when we can see that this is so, and we should be deeply thankful and worship when we gain an insight into his working.

We need to remember also that God can take and use the most unlikely people to fulfil his purposes. Who would have imagined that it would be Judah who would become the one who would demonstrate unmistakably to Joseph the change which had taken place in his own heart and in the hearts of his brothers concerning Jacob and Benjamin? Who would have imagined that the change in his life would take place in the way that it did, through a sordid and very unhappy event? We are not all like heartless Judah in his early days, but we all know what it is to be jealous of the privileges of others, to be upset if we think we are being treated unfairly, especially if this takes place within the family. We can all display a callous attitude towards the needs of others. We all need to experience the humiliation of repentance before a holy God. We all need the Lord to take us in hand and to mould and improve our characters. And we should be thankful when he does so, even though the process may be painful.

Judah and his future (Gen. 49:8–12)

W e have now looked at almost all the events in Judah's life that are recorded in the Bible. His name naturally occurs in the list of Jacob's family in Genesis 46:8–27. There is, however, one significant note in 46:28: 'He [i.e. Jacob] had sent Judah ahead of him to Joseph to show the way before him in Goshen, and they came into the land of Goshen.' Jacob here recognizes the part that Judah had played, both in persuading him to send Benjamin to Egypt, and also in interceding with Joseph on behalf of Benjamin. So Judah again becomes the go-between. He goes on ahead of the family, which naturally would travel at a more leisurely pace. Presumably Judah would have gone to Joseph, who would then have shown him where in Goshen the family were to settle. Afterwards Judah would have returned to meet up with the family group and to lead them to the place which would become their home.

It is just a sentence, but it shows the appreciation Jacob had for what his son had done. It shows, too, that Judah was the best one to go back to Joseph and make the arrangements with him for the family. We easily overlook the part that Judah played in the drama that is unfolded in these chapters in Genesis. Clearly, however, Jacob did not, and nor did Joseph.

There is only one more mention of Judah in Genesis, and that comes at the end of Jacob's life. He gathered his sons about him, knowing that the end of his life was near. He then proceeded to bless them all, 'blessing each with the blessing suitable to him' (49:28), in the course of which he also prophesied of the future of their descendants. The longest blessing is that given to Joseph (49:22–26), but the second-longest is Judah's (vv. 8–12). It is to this that we must give our attention.

Two general points can be made about these blessings. Firstly, they look to the future. Verse 1 says, 'Then Jacob called his sons and said, "Gather yourselves together, that I may tell you what shall happen to you in days to come."' It is easy to see that this does not simply refer to the days of the sons themselves, but also includes the future of the families—in fact, the tribes—that would come from them. At the same time, the starting point is often some characteristic of the son concerned. We shall see this as we look at what Jacob has to say about Judah:

Judah, your brothers shall praise you;
>   your hand shall be on the neck of your enemies;
>   your father's sons shall bow down before you.
Judah is a lion's cub;
>   from the prey, my son, you have gone up.
He stooped down; he crouched as a lion
>   and as a lioness; who dares rouse him?
The sceptre shall not depart from Judah,
>   nor the ruler's staff from between his feet,
until tribute comes to him;
>   and to him shall be the obedience of the peoples.
Binding his foal to the vine
>   and his donkey's colt to the choice vine
he has washed his garments in wine
>   and his vesture in the blood of grapes.
His eyes are darker than wine,
>   and his teeth whiter than milk. (49:8–12)

Jacob begins by focusing on the meaning of Judah's name, 'Praise' (v. 8). It was Leah who had given this name to her fourth son, saying, 'This time I will praise the LORD' (29:35). The appropriateness of this name is striking as we have considered Judah's life. What cause there was to praise God for the great change that came over him by God's grace! How much cause Jacob, Joseph, Benjamin and all the brothers had for praising the Lord for the role that Judah was enabled to play in the events leading up to the removal of Jacob and his family to Goshen! However, when Jacob says 'your brothers shall praise you', he is not simply speaking about the present; he is looking towards the 'days to come'. This is a prophecy that Judah will become the leading tribe in Israel; indeed, in a certain sense, Judah will become Israel. At the end of verse 8 we have a striking reversal of fortunes. When Jacob says 'your father's sons shall bow down before you', he is actually using the language of Joseph's dreams in 37:5–11. This is something that we will take up later, but it is unmistakably clear that Judah will eventually take the place of Joseph.

Between the two phrases just considered comes this: 'your hand shall be on the neck of your enemies.' This is simply a vivid way of saying that the tribe of Judah will be victorious; it will reach a position of pre-eminence and domination over all enemies. The fulfilment of this came about especially during the reign of David, which was followed, in its early days at least, by the peace and prosperity of Solomon's reign (1 Kings 4:20–34). At that time, too, all the other tribes, 'brothers' of Judah and sons of Jacob, owed their freedom and happiness to the goodness of God mediated through David and the tribe to which he belonged.

Genesis 49:9 is simply repeating verse 8 metaphorically. Judah is pictured as a lion's cub, a lion and a lioness (or possibly an 'old lion', KJV). There is progress over the years as the tribe grows and achieves its prominent position. In its early days it learns the secret of victory. Later it is like a crouching lion ready to attack when threatened (compare Num. 24:9). The final picture is of a lioness with cubs, which she will defend with fury. Who dares arouse a lioness looking after her little ones? We must keep this picture of a lion in mind; it will come again later on. While this illustration is taken from a natural world which was familiar to Jacob and to his descendants, we must not overlook the spiritual significance which lies behind the future flourishing of Judah. Judah himself was changed in an amazing way by the grace of God, and God was at work in all that happened to bring Israel into Egypt. David was 'a man after [God's] own heart' (1 Sam. 13:14; Acts 13:22). In his early days Solomon, too, was a man of prayer who built the temple for God's glory. While these were instruments used by the Lord, they were all men who became what they were by the grace and power of God. The rise and prosperity of the tribe of Judah were rooted in the faith and righteousness of its leaders.

The essential point of verse 10 is that Judah will become the royal tribe; that is to say, it is from this tribe that the king will come. This has already been anticipated in our referring to David and Solomon, but we need to remember that when Jacob gave his prophecy, all that was hundreds of years in the future. Jacob had a large family but it was not then a nation by any stretch of the imagination. It was gradually welded into a united people by mutual suffering in Egypt and by the exodus, but it remained very much a group of tribes until Saul was appointed the first king, and it was only under David that it really became a nation and a force to be reckoned with.

There is considerable debate about the precise understanding and meaning of verse 10. It is generally agreed, though, that it looks forward to the coming of the Messiah—God's king. The second phrase, 'nor the ruler's staff from between his feet', appears to refer to an unbroken line of rulers being born to the tribe of Judah, in this way paralleling the first clause. With the defeat of Judah by Nebuchadnezzar and the exile it looked as if this promise would not be kept. Even with the return of the exiles and the rebuilding of Jerusalem and its temple, the continuing subjugation of Judah under the Greeks and Romans made it appear that there would never again be a ruler from David's line. However, this proved to be an important transition period, for the King yet to come would be very different from the kings of the past.

In spite of the long intervening years the royal line continued until there was born in the city of David one of David's house and lineage, Jesus, the Saviour, who is Christ the Lord. Many in Judah at that time were still longing and looking for another David: a warrior king who would defeat their enemies and grant them freedom and prosperity. Few would have ever imagined that the village carpenter of Nazareth, notwithstanding his ancestry, would turn out to be the One they were expecting. Nor did they understand the nature of his kingdom when he began his ministry. His was the kingdom of heaven, the kingdom of God that would begin as he gathered around him those who would entrust themselves to him and follow him unreservedly.

The final line of verse 10 looks beyond the tribe of Judah and the nation itself when it speaks of 'the peoples' (compare 17:16; Deut. 32:8). The climactic King of the line of Judah has a kingdom which is not confined to one nation but includes within itself those from all the peoples of the earth. So it was that the King himself commissioned his eleven Judean apostles: 'Go therefore and make disciples of all nations, baptizing them in the name of the Father and of the Son and of the Holy Spirit, teaching them to observe all that I have commanded you' (Matt. 28:19–20). Verses 11 and 12 are simply a picture of the extravagant and overwhelming goodness and joy of that kingdom (compare Amos 9:13–15). Derek Kidner says: 'Every line of these verses speaks of exuberant, intoxicating abundance: it is the golden age of the Coming One … Jesus announced the age to come in just this imagery in His first "sign" at Cana of Galilee.'[1]

While it is important to see the hand of God in this story, we must not overlook the importance of Judah himself and what he did. Because of his awakening to his own sinfulness and the change that took place in him he was able to play so well the vital part that he did in reconciling Joseph and his brothers and reuniting them all with Jacob in Egypt. In taking the responsibility that he did and putting his own freedom, and possibly life itself, in jeopardy by becoming surety for Benjamin, he actually accomplished far more than he could have realized. As a result, he was given a position and played a part in the unfolding purposes of God that we can see, though he was never able to during his life.

None of us knows what hangs upon our faithful fulfilment of our responsibilities to our Lord and to our brothers and sisters in Christ. None of us knows what link in a chain we may prove to be by faithful Christian service that may seem ordinary and mundane, or may be as delicate and testing as Judah's task in speaking to Joseph on Benjamin's behalf. None of us knows what simple faithfulness and obedience to our Lord Jesus Christ may accomplish for the glory of God and the furtherance of the gospel. The call to faithful service is, however, clear and urgent.

Postscript

There is one other passage in the Old Testament that must not be overlooked in considering the line that runs from Judah to Jesus, and that is Ruth 4:11–12. When Boaz publicly bought a field from Naomi and with the field bought Ruth to be his wife, we read:

> Then all the people who were at the gate and the elders said, 'We are witnesses. May the LORD make the woman, who is coming into your house, like Rachel and Leah, who together built up the house of Israel. May you act worthily in Ephrathah and be renowned in Bethlehem, and may your house be like the house of Perez, whom Tamar bore to Judah, because of the offspring that the LORD will give you by this young woman.'

The first thing that strikes anyone who reads this is that the people of Bethlehem did not show any shame or reluctance in mentioning 'Perez, whom Tamar bore to Judah'. Nor did they show either of these attitudes as they saw Boaz betroth himself to a Moabitess. Quite the reverse: they seem to have seen both of these as events that the LORD had brought about, and they desired the LORD's blessing upon the union of Boaz and Ruth. They had clearly come to the conclusion that what had happened in the case of Judah was in the purposes of God, and their acceptance of a son born of an illicit union between their ancestor (note Ruth 1:1–2: 'Bethlehem in Judah') and a Canaanite followed from that. According to Deuteronomy 23:3, 'No Ammonite or Moabite may enter the assembly of the LORD. Even to the tenth generation …' Quite how these words would relate to a woman like Ruth may be uncertain, but the people of Bethlehem showed no prejudice or antagonism to her at all.

It is important to note that only twice in the book of Ruth are we told of the LORD acting. The first occasion comes in 1:6: 'The LORD had visited his people and given them food.' It was news of this act of God that brought Naomi and Ruth to Bethlehem. The second occasion is recorded after the wedding of Boaz and Ruth: 'the LORD gave her [Ruth] conception, and she bore a son' (4:13). So the LORD answered the prayers of the people of Bethlehem. But, as the narrative goes on to explain, this son was Obed, who became the father of Jesse, who, of course, was the father of David. It is quite clear that the main purpose of the book of Ruth is to show that in the good purposes of the LORD it was through Boaz and Ruth that the line would run that led to King David.

However, that was also the line that ran on from David and eventually to the birth of Jesus Christ in Bethlehem, the city of David. So several hundred years after the event we find Judah, Tamar and their son Perez mentioned in a passage about the birth of a son—not born through a Canaanite woman this time, but by a Moabitess. The Bible seems to go out of its way to emphasize that those from outside the chosen nation are found in the messianic line—surely indicating that Christ has come for people of all nations and from every kind of background.

NOTE

1 Derek Kidner, *Genesis*, Tyndale Old Testament Commentaries (London: Inter-Varsity Press, 1973 [1967]), p. 219.

Judah chosen as leader

I t is very easy to think of Genesis 37–50, the final chapters of the book, as the story of Joseph. He is, quite clearly, the main character. Moreover, his faithfulness to God and the blessing of God upon his life are evident and striking: 'The LORD was with Joseph, and he became a successful man, and he was in the house of his Egyptian master. His master saw that the LORD was with him and that the LORD caused all that he did to succeed in his hands' (39:2–3). He was outstanding in his resistance to temptation, in suffering frequent, undeserved setbacks, and yet rising again through his faithful trust in God and the LORD's goodness to him.

Joseph is sometimes looked upon as a spoiled brat in his youth because of what we read in chapter 37. That Jacob was unwise in his favouritism is undoubtedly true, but the only evidence we have in that chapter of Joseph's own character is that he told the dreams he had received to the rest of his family. This might have been through naivety, or it might have been boastfulness. It also might have been the natural thing to do with dreams that made a particular impression upon him and which he may well have suspected had been given by God—as indeed it turned out they were. At any rate, after he had been sold into Egypt, his wisdom as a man upon whom the Spirit of God rested (41:38–39) is both described and stated.

In 1 Chronicles 5:1–2 we find explained the rather complex situation that came about in Jacob's family:

The sons of Reuben the firstborn of Israel (for he was the firstborn, but because he defiled his father's bed, his birthright was given to the sons of Joseph the son of Israel, so that he could not be enrolled as the oldest son; though Judah became strong among his brothers and a chief came from him, yet the birthright belonged to Joseph) …

So the birthright was taken away from Reuben and transferred to Joseph and then to his son Manasseh. Mention is made of Judah, but there is only a hint of what was to come.

If for the moment we overlook Genesis 49, which we have just considered, there would be every reason to consider that it would be the tribe of Joseph which would rise to pre-eminence. Even chapter 49 looks ahead to future prosperity for Joseph's descendants:

Joseph is a fruitful bough,
    a fruitful bough by a spring;
    his branches run over the wall …
The blessings of your father
    are mighty beyond the blessings of my parents,
    up to the bounties of the everlasting hills.
May they be on the head of Joseph,
    and on the brow of him who was set apart from his brothers. (vv. 22, 26)

When we compare the growth and development of the tribes we find that Joseph's two sons, Ephraim and Manasseh, both became the progenitors of significant tribes in Israel. In Numbers 1:32–35 we are told that the tribe of Ephraim numbered 40,500 people and Manasseh 32,200, making a total of 72,700, a substantial number. This combined total was exceeded only by the tribe of Judah, with 74,600 people (Num. 1:26–27). The census recorded in Numbers 1 was taken at the beginning of the forty-year period that Israel spent in the wilderness. We might note that when the tribes were allocated to their positions around the tabernacle in the camp, Judah was mentioned first and stationed on the east of the tabernacle. This meant that it was the tribe of Judah that led the way on the march towards Canaan. This is the only hint—and it is barely that—that Judah might become the leading tribe (see Num. 2:1–4; 10:11–14). In the census taken prior to Israel entering the promised land, the tribe of Judah was much the same in number: 76,500. However, the combined total of Ephraim and Manasseh had now reached 85,200 (Num. 26). So it looked as if the Joseph tribes were going to become dominant when Israel settled in the land.

However, God does not simply take account of the largest number or of the strongest tribe. Psalm 78:67–68 says: 'He rejected the tent of Joseph; he did not choose the tribe of Ephraim, but he chose the tribe of Judah, Mount Zion, which he loves.' When Israel settled in the land that had been Canaan, Manasseh had large tracts of territory on both sides of the river Jordan. Ephraim had a smaller area in the centre of the land, while Judah occupied a large part of the south. The tribe of Simeon had an area inside Judah's allotment, which resulted in Simeon being absorbed by Judah. Benjamin had a small area between Judah and Ephraim. It is interesting

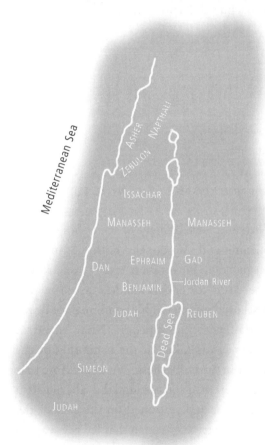

to remember that Israel's first king, Saul, belonged to Benjamin (1 Sam. 9:1–2). We might note in passing that another Saul, born in Tarsus, was also a Benjamite (Phil. 3:5). While the tribe of Benjamin also became part of Judah, it is clear that the tribal roots of its members were retained.

Once David became king, the tribe of Judah achieved pre-eminence. David himself was to say, 'Yet the LORD God of Israel chose me from all my father's house to be king over Israel for ever. For he chose Judah as leader, and in the house of Judah my father's house, and among my father's sons he took pleasure in me to make me king over all Israel'' (1 Chr. 28:4).

However, because of the foolish behaviour of David's grandson Rehoboam (1 Kings 12), the nation divided into two. The north, which was always the larger, was generally called Israel, though it is sometimes called Ephraim and occasionally Joseph (see Amos 5:6, 15). The south simply became known as Judah. It retained the capital city, Jerusalem, the place where the temple had been built and therefore the place where God had put his name (compare Deut. 12). However understandable may have been Israel's rebellion which took place under Jeroboam, what happened next was a catastrophic sin. In order to prevent Israelites going up to the temple and the worship of the LORD in Jerusalem, Jeroboam made two shrines for worship. The idolatry which this introduced marked the commencement of a long period of spiritual decline that came to its climax when the Assyrians captured Samaria, and the people of the north were removed into captivity and absorbed by the nations where they were placed (2 Kings 17).

So it was that the tribe of Judah, which first gave the whole nation King David and then King Solomon, became a nation in its own right; one which, through many vicissitudes, has continued down to this day. When we look at the northern kingdom of Israel we see God's justice. That kingdom went further and further away from their covenant LORD; there was coup and counter-coup, idolatry and bloodshed. Prophets like Amos were not heeded and eventually the nation was brought to an end.

Though God himself knows what happened to the people of Israel who were deported and who intermarried and intermingled with the other peoples within the Assyrian empire, such knowledge is hidden from us. Here were a people who were justly rejected by God for their sin of covenant unfaithfulness.

When we look at Judah we see God's grace. No one would have anticipated that Judah the son of Jacob would have become the man that he did, or that the fourth son of Leah would be the progenitor of the royal dynasty; nor that his tribe would rise to become the covenant nation, absorbing Simeon and Benjamin and such from the other tribes who came to live in the land that took his name. Yet this was what happened. In due course, however, the nation of Judah became as unfaithful as faithless Israel had been—but although there was judgement, God preserved a remnant. They had to pass through the rigours and sorrows of the destruction of Jerusalem and exile in Babylon, until after seventy years the exiles began to return, resettle in the land and rebuild Jerusalem and the temple. They remained a small nation and were subject first to the Greeks and then the Romans. Nevertheless, God preserved them, for he had purposes of grace, not just for them, but for the whole world through them. Truly, God's thoughts are not our thoughts, nor his ways, our ways (Isa. 55:8–9). He throws the 'law of primogeniture' out of the window: it was the fourth son of Jacob, born to Leah, not to Rachel, who gave the covenant nation its kings and whose line and people were preserved down the ages.

Judah in the New Testament (Matt. 1:1–17; 2:1–12; Heb. 7; Rev. 5; 7:1–8)

Matthew 1:1–17

Judah is mentioned at the very beginning of the New Testament in Matthew 1:2–3. We have already noted these remarkable words: '… Judah the father of Perez and Zerah by Tamar, and Perez the father of Hezron'. This is the third generation on from Abraham, and the genealogy leads directly to 'Jacob the father of Joseph the husband of Mary, of whom Jesus was born, who is called Christ' (v. 16).

This genealogy is astonishing. Five women are mentioned in it. Mary herself was unmarried when Jesus was conceived by the Holy Spirit. Two of the other women were from the nations with which the Israelites were forbidden to intermarry: Rahab was a Canaanite and Ruth was a Moabitess. The 'wife of Uriah' (v. 6) was, of course, Bathsheba, with whom David committed adultery before having her husband killed in battle and taking her as his wife. The fifth woman is Tamar, almost certainly a Canaanite. Her son was conceived through intercourse with her father-in-law when she pretended to be a prostitute!

None of this should be understood as in any way justifying sin and disobedience to God's commands, or as suggesting that he is indifferent when such acts take place. Rather this magnifies the grace of God who sent his own Son into a world of sinful behaviour to become the only Saviour from sin and judgement. The very way in which the line developed that would bring Jesus into the world underlined how essential it was that he should come. It would be utterly unrealistic to imagine that

Jesus could have come into the world through a line of perfect people—no such line existed or could exist. We might think that he could at least have come through a line of outwardly decent people who were marked out as godly, but that would be a great mistake on our part. It may well be that what to us are not such serious sins—and all have sinned—are viewed differently in the eyes of God. Who are we to say that pride, self-righteousness and complacency are not as serious as sexual sins or as marrying unbelievers?

The fact that five women are mentioned in the genealogy makes them stand out and makes it easy for us to recall who they were and what they were like. However, when we begin to look at the men named in this list, we soon call to mind the faults of many of them as well. Who was the greatest sinner, David or Bathsheba? What about Solomon and all his wives and concubines? Doesn't Scripture bring before us the sins of Abraham, Isaac, Jacob and Judah as well as Tamar? And, looking at the female names again, though Rahab and Ruth were both from outside the covenant people, what is noteworthy about them is the remarkable faith they each showed in the LORD, the God of Israel.

In addition to noting the way this passage magnifies the grace of God we must also see that God often does not act in the ways that we might expect him to. Just as a wicked man like Judah was brought to repentance and became an instrument in the hand of God, so God also uses outsiders in the fulfilment of his purposes. While the line is traced through the males, yet God highlights women also. Three of them are actually noted for their great faith, while the other two, Tamar and Bathsheba, were both badly misused by men. They were sinners too, of course, but in spite of how they were treated God fulfilled his purpose through them. We need to note these things because this is what we still find as the work of God continues in the world. The treasure of the gospel is brought to the world through those who can be described as 'jars of clay' (2 Cor. 4:7).

This does not justify any of us in being careless about holiness of life and behaviour. It would be better if all Christians were more devoted to Christ and exhibited greater conformity to his example. However, if the work of God continued through Christians like that, we would all tend to start taking some of the credit to ourselves. We would become pleased with our own spirituality and be in danger of taking some of the glory that belongs to God alone. So God humbles us by using those who seem unworthy in our eyes. It is a necessary lesson that we often fail to learn—indeed, we scarcely realize that there is such a lesson to learn.

Matthew 2:1–12

It is not long before the name of Judah occurs again in the New Testament. In Matthew 2 we are told of the wise men who came from the east seeking the king of the Jews. The chief priests and scribes knew exactly where to look, quoting Micah 5:2:

And you, O Bethlehem, in the land of Judah,
   are by no means least among the rulers of Judah;
for from you shall come a ruler
   who will shepherd my people Israel. (Matt. 2:6)

If you compare this verse with Micah 5:2, you will discover there is a difference. Micah says, 'But you, O Bethlehem Ephrathah, who are too little to be among the clans of Judah ...' Calvin says about this, 'We must always observe the rule, that as often as the Apostles quote a testimony from Scripture, although they do not render it word for word, in fact may move quite a way from it, they adapt it suitably and appropriately for the case in hand.'[1]

Micah is drawing attention to the fact that Bethlehem was unimportant among the clans of Judah; Matthew brings out the implication that Bethlehem became important because a ruler was to come from there. Micah, of course, prophesied long after David, the son of Jesse the

Bethlehemite, had become king. Therefore he was looking forward to someone like David but even greater. The main point for us to notice is this: God was not going to raise up the ruler who would shepherd his people Israel out of Jerusalem or any of the large cities in Judah. He would choose a small out-of-the-way place like Bethlehem. Once again we see that God's ways are not like ours. He chose Judah, the unimportant fourth son of Leah, to continue the line of the Messiah. And he chose Bethlehem, similarly unimportant, as the place where first David and then Jesus himself would be born. 'God chose what is foolish in the world to shame the wise; God chose what is weak in the world to shame the strong; God chose what is low and despised in the world, even things that are not, to bring to nothing things that are, so that no human being might boast in the presence of God' (1 Cor. 1:27–29).

Matthew adds in his quotation some words that come a little later in the passage from Micah:

And he shall stand and shepherd his flock in the strength of the LORD,
in the majesty of the name of the LORD his God.
And they shall dwell secure, for now he shall be great
to the ends of the earth.
And he shall be their peace. (Micah 5:4–5)

The security spoken of here arises because this ruler's influence will extend to 'the ends of the earth'. He will bring peace wherever his reign extends. This is a clear prophecy of the fact that the kingdom of this ruler, Jesus Christ the King, will be worldwide. The inclusion of people from all the nations of the world will eventually result in new heavens and a new earth where people from every nation, tribe and tongue will be united in worship, thanksgiving and service (Rev. 7:9–12).

Revelation 7 itself proceeds to a glorious climax, also picking up the shepherd theme of Micah:

Therefore they are before the throne of God,

and serve him day and night in his temple;

and he who sits on the throne will shelter them with his presence.

They shall hunger no more, neither thirst any more;

the sun shall not strike them,

nor any scorching heat.

For the Lamb in the midst of the throne will be their shepherd,

and he will guide them to springs of living water,

and God will wipe away every tear from their eyes. (vv. 15–17)

Hebrews 7

We have been looking at verses speaking of Judah, even though it is the tribe that is being referred to, because in various respects the fortunes of the tribe reflect truths about the person from whom the tribe was descended. This is also the case when we turn to Hebrews 7:14: 'For it is evident that our Lord was descended from Judah, and in connection with that tribe Moses said nothing about priests.' Moses had been told to appoint priests from the tribe of Levi. The point that the writer is making is simply that if those priests had been able to bring about perfection— that is, full and complete forgiveness and righteousness before God— there would have been no need for a priest to come from a different tribe. But as Jesus Christ, who is our great High Priest, came from the tribe of Judah, that fact in itself tells us that the Levitical priesthood was totally inadequate for bringing in perfection. Indeed, it was never intended by God for that purpose. That priesthood was but a preparation for and shadow of the perfect priesthood that came with the Messiah.

So just as Reuben, Jacob's firstborn, and Joseph the man of God were bypassed in the purposes of God so far as the line of the Messiah was concerned, so the Levitical priesthood was also bypassed. We might have imagined that, as Jesus was to be our priest and was to offer the final, perfect sacrifice for sin, he should have been born a Levite; it would seem the natural thing from our point of view. However, in Israel, unlike many of the nations round about, there was a complete distinction between kingship and priesthood. Kings came from the line of Judah through David; priests came from the line of Levi. Kings could not usurp priestly actions and were judged by God when they did so (1 Sam. 13:1–14; 2 Chr. 26:16–23). In modern terms, church and state were kept apart as far as leadership was concerned.

Jesus Christ, however, was to be a king and priest, as well as a prophet, so his priesthood was patterned on that of Melchizedek (Heb. 7). This man was king of Salem—that is, Jerusalem—but he was not descended from Abraham at all; indeed, he was greater than Abraham (vv. 4–10). That the priesthood of Jesus was after the order of Melchizedek emphasizes the superiority of Jesus over all others, even though he himself was a descendant of Abraham and David. He became 'a priest, not on the basis of a legal requirement concerning bodily descent, but by the power of an indestructible life' (v. 16).

Here again, we see that God's methods are different from ours. Tribe and race—'bodily descent'—are not important to him in the way that they can be to us. In this case it is Christ's eternity as the Son of God—'an indestructible life'—which is the basis of his priesthood. It is as if God deliberately overthrows the way we are likely to think; he takes outsiders and the unsuitable—from our point of view—and uses them in his overall purposes of grace. One with this indestructible life is born from the line of Judah! It would take us too far from our study of Judah to pursue the line of the Levites, but if you read Genesis 34 and 49:5–7 it also seems remarkable that Levi should have been the tribe from which the priests and temple servants were to come.

Revelation 5

We are taken more directly back to Judah in Revelation 5:5: 'And one of the elders said to me, "Weep no more; behold, the Lion of the tribe of Judah, the Root of David, has conquered, so that he can open the scroll and its seven seals."' We are immediately reminded of the blessing of Jacob: 'Judah is a lion's cub; from the prey, my son, you have gone up. He stooped down; he crouched as a lion and as a lioness; who dares rouse him?' (Gen. 49:9). Here is the ultimate fulfilment of those words. There is a certain progression in the verse from Genesis: Judah begins as a cub but becomes a grown-up lion. So, after Judah himself, there is a partial fulfilment in David, a man of war, but there is a final fulfilment in this glorious Lion, who is also a Lamb (Rev. 5:6). It was in this verse that C. S. Lewis found his inspiration for Aslan in his Narnia books.

There are probably several ideas bound up in this picture of a Lion. Firstly, we should see that the emphasis is on the victory of this Lion: he 'has conquered'. But, Lion though he is, it does not appear that this conquest has been won by force. The fact that John continued to look and saw 'a Lamb standing, as though it had been slain' (v. 6) indicates that the victory was achieved by death and resurrection. Though he looked as if he had been slain, yet now he was standing: alive after death. So, having gained the victory, Jesus Christ appears as the Lion; all power is given to him and he can open the scroll of history and bring to pass all the purposes of God.

This fits in with the fact that the lion is often considered as a regal animal, the lord of the jungle. This is what Jacob's prophecy had looked forward to:, 'Judah is a lion's cub … The sceptre shall not depart from Judah' (Gen. 49:9–10). With power and authority Jesus Christ rules over the world. In a special way he is Head over his church. God has

raised him from the dead and seated him at his right hand in the heavenly places, far above all rule and authority and power and dominion, and above every name that is named, not only in this age but also in the one to come. And he put all things under his feet and gave him as head over all things to the church, which is his body, the fullness of him who fills all in all. (Eph. 1:20–23)

The tribe of Judah gave Israel King David, who won many victories and kept the people safe and secure. As a result of his conquests there followed the peace and prosperity of Solomon's reign. Today, all believers have a Lion to defend them, to assure their safety, to grant them quietness of heart and peace of mind, and to refresh and renew them spiritually day after day. Moreover, he is preparing a place of eternal rest and joy for them in the Father's house, where all the trials and tribulations of life in a sinful world will be over once and for all.

However, you cannot trifle with a lion; and you certainly cannot with this one. As stated in the prophecy of Jacob, who dares rouse a lion to anger or provoke him (Gen. 49:9)? So this picture reminds us to live humbly and honestly before our Lion King. Sin, carelessness and hardness of heart must be put away. Christ spews the lukewarm out of his mouth, and all too often he has to say that he has something against the members of his churches. He reproves and disciplines his people because he loves them, so it is important to be zealous and repent when this is necessary.

That is not the note on which we should end our consideration of the lion imagery. There is something magnificent about a lion; there is something stately about the way he walks. He seems to have no fear; his roar shakes the jungle; his mane glimmers in the sunshine; he holds his head up high. So, in his own superior way, is Jesus Christ. He is Lord, the faithful and true One, supremely glorious in his majesty and power. When John, who knew him well, saw him in all his risen, kingly excellence, he fell at his feet as though dead. And so would we if we were to have the vision that he did. Yet Jesus laid his right hand on John and said, 'Fear not' (Rev. 1:13–18). So great and exalted is the Lord of glory, yet so kind and tender: there is no king like him!

Revelation 7:1–8

The second and last reference to Judah in the book of Revelation, and therefore in the whole Bible, comes in 7:4–5: 'And I heard the number of the sealed, 144,000, sealed from every tribe of the sons of Israel: 12,000 from the tribe of Judah were sealed.' The point which is of interest here is that the tribe of Judah is listed first before all the other tribes, the only time in the Bible when this occurs. It must be admitted that it is difficult to find any reason for the order in which the tribes are listed here, but bearing in mind the earlier description of Christ as 'the Lion of the tribe of Judah', the implication seems to be that this tribe has the pre-eminence.

How this passage at the beginning of Revelation 7 is interpreted will depend on the way in which the whole book is approached. The reference to the twelve tribes here can be understood in very different ways, and this is not the place to attempt an interpretation. This passage simply seems to show what we have been seeing all along. In spite of the historical Judah's insignificance in terms of his birth, and in spite of all that the early events in his life reveal about his character for a good part of his life, he and his tribe came, by the grace of God, to a remarkable place in the unfolding of the purposes of God. Reuben was the firstborn, Levi was the father of the priests and temple servants, Joseph was outstanding personally and in the role he played for Israel in Egypt; but in the end it is Judah's name and tribe which reach the first place of honour. His name will never perish from the earth. The Lord God has seen to that.

NOTE

1 John Calvin, *A Harmony of the Gospels* (Edinburgh: St Andrew Press, 1972), p. 85.

Why Judah and not Joseph?

We considered earlier that in God's purposes it was from the line of Judah that Jesus Christ was to be born, rather than from the line of Joseph. However, this is so unexpected that it requires us to look more closely and see if we can discern any reasons for it. It is not just that Joseph has such a prominent place in the later chapters of Genesis; it is also very difficult to read the life of Joseph without noticing that there are many parallels with the life of Jesus, so much so that older writers on the Bible generally saw Joseph as a 'type' or picture of Jesus Christ.

For example, Henry Law wrote this about Joseph:

The Scripture before us is precious, because every view of Joseph exhibits Jesus. Who is the envied, and hated, and rejected of his brethren? Who is the sold for pieces of silver; the cast out into Egypt; the numbered with the transgressors; the apparent culprit between two offenders; of whom one is exalted, the other perishes? Who is raised from the prison to the right hand of majesty? In all these outlines, is not Jesus seen? He it is on whose shoulder the government is laid. He it is, who rescues his own kindred from perishing. He it is, whose heart yearned over them, when they knew him not. He it is, to whom the perishing must flee. He it is, who has the key of all supplies. His name is Joseph. The true image is Jesus.[1]

In another book Law says of Joseph's appearance in Genesis 37:

Instantly the type shows Jesus. The Father's voice from heaven proclaims, 'This is my beloved Son'; Matt. 3:17. The Spirit witnesses, 'Thy holy child Jesus'; Acts 4:27. 'Thou lovest righteousness and hatest iniquity'; Psalm 45:7.

And a little later he goes on to speak of Judah:

Now merchants appear journeying towards Egypt. Judah reasons, our brother dying in the pit is gainless. His blood, too, will accuse. To sell him is a present profit and less guilt. He will live, and we, unstained by blood, shall be enriched. Consent is ready. The bargain is made. Twenty silver coins are paid. Joseph is carried down to Egypt. Who can see Judah's covetous desire, and not discern the traitor Judas![2]

More recent writers are not so likely to express things in quite so direct a way, but it is certainly true that there are many parallels between the life of Joseph and that of Jesus Christ. Nor can it be a mistake to draw out these parallels and indicate that the God whose grace is so evident in the life of Joseph is the same God who gave his own Son to bring about an even greater salvation than Joseph's deliverance of his family. However, it would be a mistake to assume that, because the life of Joseph has its parallels in aspects of the life and ministry of the Lord Jesus, Jesus ought to have been born from Joseph's line. This does not follow, and neither is it necessarily fitting. So are there any reasons why Jesus should have been born from Judah's line, rather than Joseph's?

First of all, we have to acknowledge the sovereignty of God in this matter. It is not appropriate for us even to question what God has done, though we may reverently consider possible reasons for his actions. If we were to find no other reason at all than his sovereignty, that should be sufficient for us. God's ways are not to be questioned by his creatures. He chose the line of Judah, and that is sufficient.

This choice does, however, fit in with the fact that the Son of God humbled himself when he came into the world (Phil. 2:1–8). Today, tracing one's ancestors has become the interest of very many people, but it sometimes brings shocks and uncovers realities in our family tree that we might wish had never happened. We can be humbled by discovering illegitimate births, criminal ancestors, suicides and terrible poverty or cruelty. But that is life in a fallen world, and it was into such a world that the Son of God came. We might have wished him to have had the sort of family tree that we would like: decent, respectable, good-living people—sinners, yes, but nice, genteel sinners, not at all the nasty type!

However, the differences between human sinners are marginal compared with the difference between all sinners and the holy Son of God. In a sense, the story of Judah simply reminds us of that. For the Son to be born of a human mother and take our nature was a self-humbling that we cannot measure, but to look at his family tree enables us to gain some indication of it. Moreover, this should also serve to humble us. We belong to the same tribe of sinners that Judah did, and so do all the other evil men and women that we read of in the Bible and see around us every day. We are humbled, too, when we realize what it meant for the Son of God to come into this world for our salvation. Judah is our relative as well as Jesus' ancestor. We were all one in sin, and it is by grace that we receive the same forgiveness and change that Judah experienced.

We have to remember, also, that Jesus identified himself with sinful people. Although he himself was sinless, he was baptized with a baptism of repentance for the forgiveness of sins (Luke 3:3). He stood in the place of sinful people because he himself was going to take the punishment of sin upon the cross. It was the respectable and religious who rejected him; it was the tax collectors and prostitutes who believed John the Baptist and him (Matt. 21:31–32). It was the Judahs of this world who were among the most responsive to his ministry. Joseph was a man whose power was second only to that of Pharaoh, but Judah was a suppliant, pleading on behalf of others—Benjamin and his father—identifying himself with his half-brother, and willing to substitute himself for him.

It is also fitting that Jesus should have been born in the line of one who experienced a remarkable change of character and life. That Joseph needed forgiveness and the grace of God can be taken for granted, but in the case of Judah it is exemplified to a remarkable degree. He is a monument of grace. The change from his vicious condemnation of Tamar to his plea to Joseph for Benjamin and Jacob is monumental and shows what God can do. It was for this reason that the Son of God came into the world: to save sinners; and that means not only forgiveness but also transformation. In this respect, Judah is a sort of visual aid in the way that Joseph cannot be.

It is important not to make unfair comparisons between Joseph and Judah. They both figure in the ongoing story of God's grace, playing the separate parts that God had for each. Both, in various ways, point towards the Lord Jesus Christ. There is much to learn from each of them. It *could* have been the will of God for Jesus to have been born from Joseph's line, but in fact it was not. There is value, though, in seeing what makes it appropriate for Jesus to have been born from Judah's line: it helps us magnify the grace of God.

NOTES

1 Henry Law, *The Gospel in Genesis* (London: Banner of Truth Trust, 1960), p. 169.
2 Henry Law, *Beacons of the Bible* (London: James Nisbet & Co, 1865), pp. 241, 244.

Judah and us today

T his chapter is not concerned with the descendants of the tribe of Judah after the time of Jesus Christ, nor with how these might relate to today's Israel. Its intention is to see how the story of Judah can be applied to all those who believe in Jesus Christ in the twenty-first century, no matter their nationality or background. It is the spiritual significance that is of the greatest importance.

The first thing that stands out in the chapters in Genesis that we have been looking at is the heartbreaking foolishness of human sinful behaviour. What sorrow and misery were brought into their family by the fact that Isaac and Rebekah each had a favourite son! How evil and counter-productive was Jacob's grasping for what belonged to Esau and the resulting deception of his father. It was this covetous desire that changed the course of Jacob's life and plunged him into the vortex of unhappiness and sorrow that lasted for so much of it. What harm Laban did by his deceitful 'gift' of Leah to Jacob, poisoning his daughters' family life, introducing envy and hatred among his grandchildren! And Judah himself, hard-hearted, despising the covenant line and marrying a Canaanite, producing two evil sons whom God removed by death, lying to Tamar, neglecting her and thus provoking her to an immoral act in which he himself unknowingly participated!

The story of Judah is located first in Canaan and then in Egypt. Both of these were pagan cultures. The ancient patriarchs did not live in a land and kingdom dedicated to the LORD, nor did they live in a culture greatly influenced by faith in him. They had to live for God in the midst of idolatrous people whose values and practices were very far from pleasing to God. It was not easy for them to resist the pressures to conform to the culture that predominated all around them; they needed grace from God and determination of heart if they were going to live God-honouring lives. More and more in the Western world we find ourselves similarly living in an atheistic, immoral society and confronting much the same challenges and temptations that came to Judah.

His world is the world that we know and experience. All around us are men and women who bring distress and bitterness into their own lives and the lives of one another by their selfishness or their desires for money, fame or sex. And we are all like that: we all share the same nature, we all have the same evil, self-centred, God-disobeying potential within us. We spoil our own lives, we hurt the ones we love, we lead others astray by our example, we sow seeds that produce a bitter harvest. 'Do not be deceived: God is not mocked, for whatever one sows, that will he also reap. For the one who sows to his own flesh will from the flesh reap corruption, but the one who sows to the Spirit will from the Spirit reap eternal life' (Gal. 6:7–8). 'Flesh' here does not mean the body; it means the principle of evil that is deep within the heart of each of us.

It is not enough simply to bemoan what is going on in the world; what about the churches? The trouble is that as Christian people we often fail; we too frequently allow the evil in our hearts to modify, if not entirely determine, our behaviour. So we find the marriages of Christians under pressure, children who have bad examples set before them in the home, poor witnesses in the workplace, and disunity and carnal attitudes within church life itself. Thank God that there is the possibility of repentance; there is real and full forgiveness through the saving death of Jesus Christ; there is renewed grace and power from the Holy Spirit. There is also the need to watch and pray, to be ruthless with ourselves in dealing with our own particular weaknesses and besetting sins. 'Put to death therefore what is earthly in you: sexual immorality, impurity, passion, evil desire, and covetousness, which is idolatry' (Col. 3:5).

Is it not true that we ought to pray more about family life? After all, it is the family that in so many ways moulds the lives of its children. We should pray for Christian families; it is not easy to bring up children in the days in which we live. We should pray for children brought up in families that are broken in various ways. What a terrible start in life some children sadly experience: abuse, drunkenness, marriage breakdown—if marriage has actually taken place. Though there are other things that believers and churches can do with sensitivity and love—and many churches have parents and toddler groups, Sunday school, youth activities and so on—earnest, thoughtful prayer is something that all can engage in and is always a vital priority.

The story of Judah also reminds us that we cannot anticipate what God is going to do. We all tend to have our own ideas of the way God will work; sometimes we think we know how God should work. Yet again and again as we read the Bible we are surprised by the way he actually does work and, if we have our eyes open, at the way he still works in the present. Some churches grow and flourish in spite of problems within them and superficiality; others, which appear to have dedicated members who work hard in a variety of ministries, seem to be static. Christian parents who take care to bring up their children in the faith find them slipping away when they grow older, while young people without any Christian background are wonderfully converted and grow up into fine men and women of God.

The fact is that we all have to be humble before God; he is our Lord and Master and his way is always the best. We cannot, and must not, set out in our minds how he ought to work. Of course, we are to follow what he tells us in his Word, and we can expect him to honour the promises we find there; but how, and when and in what way—all that is in his hands. Moreover, we have to try to take a long-term view. Jacob thought that his son by Rachel, Joseph, was lost to him. He may well have thought that Judah was lost to him as well, in quite a different way. But in neither case were things as they seemed. Joseph was not dead and after many years they met again. Judah became a changed man and it was through him that this reunion took place. Jacob lived to see the day that brought the joyous surprise into his life; who knows what joyous surprises may await us in the future, and especially in eternity?

At the end of his life Jacob called his sons to him, blessed them 'each with the blessing suitable to him' (Gen. 49:28) and told each of them 'what shall happen to you in days to come' (v. 1). Those 'days to come' went far beyond the lives of the sons themselves as, by the Holy Spirit's guidance, Jacob spoke of the tribes that would grow from his sons' families. We have already considered what he said about the future of Judah. Jacob could never, however, have imagined exactly how Judah's legacy would develop. Implicit in his prophecy was the coming of the Son of God in human nature, born of Judah's line. How astonished Jacob would surely have been if he could have foreseen how the fulfilment of his prophecy would take place and what it actually entailed! We should marvel at God's ways at the same time as we humble ourselves before him, for, as he said,

my thoughts are not your thoughts,
    neither are your ways my ways …
For as the heavens are higher than the earth,
    so are my ways higher than your ways
    and my thoughts than your thoughts. (Isa. 55:8–9)

It is true that Judah grew up in a household with tensions and even hatred. We can see that he had severe disadvantages and that it is not altogether surprising that he became the sinful, hard-hearted man that the Bible shows him to have been. Yet the fact that he was changed and became so different gives us hope. By the grace of God, people can rise above their circumstances; they can be set free from the hurts of the past and the downward spiral of an ungodly life. We have a gospel which tells us that this is so. We have a Saviour who is able to deliver men and women, young and old, from the chains that have gradually wound themselves around their hearts and lives. We should be assured that there is hope for the worst of sinners; we can tell them with confidence that Jesus saves. They can have peace of heart and mind; they can know peace with God. They may not always be able to develop in the way that Judah did, but life can begin again, and they can have the sure and certain hope of eternal glory before them.

The example of Judah reminds us that we can never write people off or think they are beyond the reach of God's grace and power. Prodigals who go off into the far country, far from God, far from Christian influence, and sink in sinful activity of one sort or another, can return, and, in God's goodness, some do. There may sometimes come a point where it is counter-productive to try to speak about the gospel to a relative or friend. We may lose all contact with someone we knew and were once close to, but that does not mean we should ever give up all hope of their return, or their coming, to the Lord. In Jesus' parable of the prodigal son, the father was still looking out for his son, still hoping, still on the watch. What joy he felt as he rushed to welcome his son back again! The son had been lost; now he was found. It was as if he had been dead, and now he was alive again! Such happy occasions still happen today; they will still happen tomorrow.

Looking at the life of Judah we see him putting himself, his freedom and his life itself on the line for Benjamin, his father Jacob and his brothers. He did not know that the high official he had to deal with was Joseph. He must have known how arbitrary and cruel those in high places could be in those days—as, too often, in these days also. He was prepared to sacrifice himself for others, if that was the price that had to be paid. It is very seldom that Christians in the West are called to face the possibility of such a sacrifice. To our shame, however, we often baulk at the much lesser self-sacrifices that we are called to as followers of Jesus Christ. We find it hard to be true to the old adage 'Jesus first, others next, self last'.

We too easily forget that Jesus said, 'If anyone would come after me, let him deny himself and take up his cross and follow me' (Matt. 16:24).

Judah's self-sacrificing spirit naturally reminds us of the Lord Jesus himself, but it is not necessary to think of Judah himself as personally prefiguring Christ. Rather, the life of Judah reminds us of the need for a Saviour to come. The evil of his early life, his desperate need of forgiveness, the extraordinary change that took place in him: these are the things that point us towards Jesus. 'Christ Jesus came into the world to save sinners,' wrote Paul, who went on to add, 'of whom I am the foremost' (1 Tim. 1:15). Judah could have added those last words too. He himself had been forgiven and been made a new man in anticipation of Christ Jesus. How remarkable: Christ was to come through him, yet he was forgiven through Christ! That is the grace of an eternal God.

Once we closely examine the life of Judah it becomes almost impossible to overlook what happened in that life and we are led to marvel at the way he pleaded before Joseph. Judah was the first Jew and it may be that that is a good way to think of him. What a pattern he has set; what an example he has left us! In fact, the more you think about it, the more right it seems that the Saviour of sinful people should have come from the line of Judah. This man was a saved sinner *par excellence*. From the depths of his utter unworthiness to the heights of his self-sacrificial plea on behalf of Benjamin and his family we see the wonder of God's grace. His name should always remind us of the wonderful turnaround that took place in his life and should point us to the One who came from his line.